The Great Leap

by Lauren Yee

SAMUEL FRENCH

FOR PRODUCTION INQUIRIES

UNITED STATES AND CANADA
info@concordtheatricals.com
1-866-979-0447

UNITED KINGDOM AND EUROPE
licensing@concordtheatricals.co.uk
020-7054-7298

Each title is subject to availability from Concord Theatricals Corp.,
depending upon country of performance. Please be aware that THE
GREAT LEAP may not be licensed by Concord Theatricals Corp. in
your territory. Professional and amateur producers should contact the
nearest Concord Theatricals Corp. office or licensing partner to verify
availability.

THE GREAT LEAP was first produced at the Denver Center in Denver, Colorado from February 2 – March 11, 2018, and then at Seattle Rep. in Seattle, Washington from March 23 – April 22, 2018. The productions were directed by Eric Ting, with sets by Wilson Chin, lighting by Christopher Kuhl, costumes by Valérie Thérèse Bart, sound by Curtis Craig, projections by Shawn Duan, and dramaturgy by Kristin Leahey. The stage manager was Jessica Bomball, and the assistant stage manager was Dana Reiland. The cast was as follows:

MANFORD . . . . Linden Tailor
CONNIE . . . . Keiko Green
WEN CHANG . . . . Joseph Steven Yang
SAUL . . . . .Bob Ari

THE GREAT LEAP was subsequently produced by the Atlantic Theater Company in New York City from May 23 – June 17, 2018. The production was directed by Taibi Magar and assistant director Ran Xia, with sets by Takeshi Kata, lighting by Eric Southern, costumes by Tilly Grimes, sound by Broken Chord, projections by David Bengali, and movement direction by Jesse Perez. The stage manager was Laura Smith. The cast was as follows:

MANFORD . . . . Tony Vo
CONNIE . . . . .Ali Ahn
WEN CHANG . . . . .BD Wong
SAUL . . . . Ned Eisenberg

THE GREAT LEAP was commissioned by the Denver Center.

CHARACTERS

THE TEAM

MANFORD – (#1) Seventeen, male, Chinese American. Intense, scrappy, runs into trouble, attacks the rim, has a ruthless crossover. Not tall. More Allen Iverson than Jeremy Lin.

CONNIE – (#2) Twenty-five, female, Chinese American, Manford's cousin, and UC Berkeley grad student. Level-headed, big picture. A Chris Paul/Klay Thompson type.

WEN CHANG – (#3) Forty-three, male, Chinese, coach of Beijing University's men's basketball team. Observant, efficient. Favors three-pointers over aggressive inside shots. Tim Duncan would appreciate his energy. (His English is formal but relatively unaccented.)

SAUL – (#4) Fifty-two, male, Jewish, coach of University of San Francisco's men's basketball team. A shit-talking, shot-blocking, washed-up Larry Bird.

SETTING

San Francisco, California
Beijing, China

TIME

May 1989
Summer/Fall 1971 and June 1989

ABOUT THE PLAY

This is a play about basketball, but it is also a basketball play. The game is reflected not just in the subject matter, but the rhythm, structure, language, and how the characters move through space.

We also should have a sense that someone is always watching.

We may or may not see any actual basketballs onstage.

AUTHOR'S NOTES

Growing up, my father played basketball. Every day, all night, on the asphalt courts and rec center floors of San Francisco Chinatown. It was the only thing he was good at.

He was never good enough that he was going to play for the NBA or even at the college level, but for a 6'1" Chinatown kid from the projects, he was good. Really good.

I know this because even today, people still stop him on the street and try to explain to me what a legend he was. They tell me his nickname (Spider), his position (center), and his signature move (the reverse jump shot). Then they will tell me about China.

One of my dad's first trips to China was in the 80s playing a series of exhibition games against China's top teams. At their first game, my dad and his American teammates faced off against a Beijing team of three-hundred-pound seven-footers that demolished them. It was the first of many slaughters.

Today he no longer plays, but his head is still in the game. He will walk up to tall young men at checkout counters, parking lots, and sporting events and ask them if they've ever considered playing basketball. And no matter the answer, he proceeds to give them a master class in technique right then and there.

This play is not my father's story.

But it is a story like it.

Special thanks

Joshua Kahan Brody, Mark Christine, Will Davis, Francis Jue, Doug Langworthy, Brian Keane, Kevin Lin, Jo Mei, Joe Ngo, and Kent Thompson.

For
all the Jeremy Lins
(on and off the court)

Prologue

[Projection: An image flashes across a screen: an old photograph, black and white, grainy, of two basketball coaches in a handshake. And a caption that reads: "Beijing 1971."]

SAUL. *(Voice-over.)* Eighteen years, that's how long you got. You start at eighteen and you're lucky if you hit thirty-six and you can still run down the court without blowing your knees out. And you want to know why?

WEN CHANG. *(Voice-over.)* Because you Americans are always running, you can never wait your turn.

SAUL. *(Voice-over.)* It is always your turn.

Every time you are on that court, it is always your turn.

WEN CHANG. *(Voice-over.)* "It is always your turn."

(A flash, and then the image disappears.)

Scene

[Projection: "San Francisco. 1989. Eighteen years later."]

(Then we see an indoor basketball court at the University of San Francisco. **MANFORD**, *dressed in an ill-fitting black suit, reads to* **SAUL** *from his notes, very fast, almost stream of consciousness:)*

MANFORD. I will win you games.

I will score you points.

I will make you layups.

I will shoot from half-court, full-court.

I will shoot over whatever whenever whoever is getting in my way.

I am quick. I am relentless.

I am the most relentless person you have ever met and if you have met someone more relentless than me, tell me, tell me and I will meet them and I will find a way to become even more relentless than them.

I am a people person.

I am a guy's guy.

I am a man's man.

But raised by my mom, so Title IX, equal opportunity.

I carpe diem.

I think, therefore I am.

– I'm just gonna keep going till you stop me –

When you say jump, I say ten feet.

I don't drink, I don't eat, I don't breathe, that's not true, I don't know why I put that.

I live for the moment.

I am the "I" in team –

SAUL. You done yet?

MANFORD. And if you don't give me a chance, I will regret this for the rest of my life.

Or, no, you, you will regret this for the rest of your life.

I'm just going to stop now and show you what I can do.

I should've started with that.

Okay, here I go.

SAUL. Kid, what're you doing?

MANFORD. You said I had thirty seconds to tell you why I was shitting all over your practice before you had security drag me out by the balls, so I am doing just that.

SAUL. No, WHY are you here. To begin with.

MANFORD. Isn't it obvious? I'm here to join the team.

SAUL. It's May. Season's over.

MANFORD. China. China. You're going to China. In one month's time.

SAUL. Who told you that, Rain Man?

(**MANFORD** *takes out a newspaper, reads:*)

MANFORD. "I brought basketball to China, I taught Beijing the game / my visit changed everything, and now I'm ready for a rematch."

SAUL. "My visit changed everything, and now I'm ready for a rematch."

MANFORD. Saul Slezac, the American coach.

SAUL. They finally ran the interview! Where'd you find that?

MANFORD. Today's Chron, sports section. Beijing University vs. USF. Friendship game. They're gonna broadcast it on TV.

SAUL. Let me see that!

(**SAUL** *takes the newspaper.*)

They stuck me across from the obituaries. Of course.

MANFORD. So can I show you what I can do?

SAUL. You snuck into my practice.

MANFORD. I came in through the players' entrance.

SAUL. You barreled into my point guard.

MANFORD. I thought he saw me coming!

SAUL. You twisted his ankle.

MANFORD. My bad.

SAUL. Why would I "see what you can do" when you've just shown me what an inconsiderate sonofabitch you are?

MANFORD. 'Cause your point guard, Kovitsky? He's injured, he's out, and you're playing Beijing in a month. Sorry I'm late: Colma is far, the service ran long.

SAUL. What, you come from a funeral or something?

(**MANFORD** *rips off a black armband.*)

MANFORD. *(Re: clothes.)* Yes. Obviously.

SAUL. Well, my condolences –

MANFORD. It's nothing. It's no one. They're dead, doesn't matter. You're not going to find anyone as good as me on such short notice.

SAUL. "As good as you"?

MANFORD. I am the most feared player in Chinatown.

SAUL. And I'm the least circumcised Jew from the Bronx.

MANFORD. What does that mean?

SAUL. It means I'm sure you're good for a Chinese player.

MANFORD. For any player.

SAUL. But if you were black –

MANFORD. If I were black, I'd be playing in the NBA.

SAUL. And if you changed your height, your muscle mass, and every single thing about you, starting center for the Lakers, why not!

MANFORD. I'm the best in the Bay, I promise you. Ask around and you'll see.

SAUL. Ask who? Ask Chinatown?

MANFORD. Or your players.

SAUL. My players?

MANFORD. If they're straight with you, they'll tell you I've played them, I've beat them.

SAUL. You beat my guys?

MANFORD. Summer leagues, off-season, I go across the bridge to Oakland and take 'em down with my crew.

SAUL. And who is this "crew"?

MANFORD. Robert Lai, Donald Woo, Munson Jin, Dennis Jue, Kwock Yee –

SAUL. Chinese.

MANFORD. My team from Galileo.

SAUL. Galileo HIGH SCHOOL?

MANFORD. YES.

SAUL. You're telling me a high school team of Chinese kids beat my guys?

MANFORD. You are finally understanding me, YES.

SAUL. What's your name, kid?

MANFORD. Manford. / "As in Stanford."

SAUL. "As in Stanford."

MANFORD. The name was aspirational, unfortunately.

SAUL. You know what? I HAVE heard about you. Oh yeah, now I remember, my players told me about you. This loudmouth point guard from Chinatown, who runs around like some goddamn Duracell bunny.

MANFORD. And took his team all the way to city finals this year.

SAUL. But you didn't win it, did you?

MANFORD. They pulled me out in overtime.

SAUL. You mean they ejected you.

MANFORD. For BS technicals.

SAUL. The only player I've ever heard of getting thrown out of a game for fighting with his own teammates.

MANFORD. My guys weren't bringing it and someone needed to call them on their shit.

    (Beat.)

Your players could use some of that, too.

SAUL. You think you know my guys?

MANFORD. Since I BEAT them, think I know them better than you.

SAUL. So tell me then. What do you know about my guys?

MANFORD. Well, tell me who they are and I'll tell you what I know.

SAUL. Hunt.

MANFORD. Forward. Can't shoot, won't shoot, not at the right time at least, chokes on the ball when you give it to him.

SAUL. Fisher.

MANFORD. Shooting guard. I've seen eunuchs with better ball-handling skills than him.

SAUL. McKellan.

MANFORD. Lazy center, can't run, his instincts suck, doesn't know how to be a fourth-quarter man.

SAUL. Wanamaker.

MANFORD. Injured, injured, always injured.

SAUL. Jackson.

MANFORD. Ball hog. Too slow. Keep going?

(**SAUL** *slow claps.*)

You're welcome.

SAUL. And if you ACTUALLY knew my team, you would know that I go for height.

MANFORD. And because I ACTUALLY DO know your team, I ALSO know that you use height to cover for sloppy fundamentals and lazy footwork.

SAUL. That height is gonna be our advantage over the Chinese, trust me.

MANFORD. Come on, Coach, I'm a point guard. We aren't supposed to be tall!

SAUL. You're not supposed to be midgets either.

MANFORD. I'm six-two.

SAUL. Five-two.

MANFORD. Five-ten.

SAUL. Five-five at best.

MANFORD. My mom was tall, my dad was not.

SAUL. Name me four ACTUALLY GOOD point guards under six foot.

MANFORD. Calvin Murphy, Spud Webb, and Muggsy Bogues. BOOM.

SAUL. That was three. I said four. BOOM. Can you even tell me the last time USF started a point guard under six feet?

MANFORD. ...I don't know.

SAUL. Exactly. Not happening. You want to try out, come back in the fall. Or better yet, when you hit puberty.

MANFORD. I don't go here, I'm seventeen. And puberty tends to happen / around thirteen, fourteen –

SAUL. I know that. That was a joke.

MANFORD. Okay, but jokes are funny.

SAUL. This is a college game, kid. You're not even done with high school yet. You think I'm gonna run afoul of child labor laws like that?

MANFORD. I'll get permission. I'll graduate.

SAUL. Not worth the hassle.

MANFORD. USF was 8-20 this season. I am completely worth the hassle.

SAUL. Hey, I get it. I used to be just like you, a scrappy kid who wanted to play with the bigs, but even I learned to accept my biological destiny.

MANFORD. You mean the biological destiny where you stop trying to win?

SAUL. You think I don't want to win?

MANFORD. I think anyone who's satisfied with 8-20 doesn't deserve a Division One-sized paycheck.

SAUL. You watch your booster program go belly-up and you see how easy it is to retain quality players without bribing 'em hand over fist.

MANFORD. Just let me practice. If you like what you see –

SAUL. Sorry, practice is over.

MANFORD. No, it's not.

SAUL. – For you. It is over for you.

(**MANFORD** *stands in* **SAUL***'s path.*)

MANFORD. Let's make a bet. I win, I go with you to China. You win? You will never have to see me again.

SAUL. That's enticing. So what's the bet?

MANFORD. Free throws.

SAUL. How many?

MANFORD. How many you want?

SAUL. What?

MANFORD. How many baskets do you want me to sink?

SAUL. Twenty in a row?

MANFORD. How about fifty?

SAUL. How about five dozen?

MANFORD. I make a hundred straight baskets every night before bed. So you may want to be more ambitious than that.

SAUL. You're going to shoot me a hundred free throws? Without a miss?

MANFORD. YES.

SAUL. You do that and I am definitely taking you to China.

MANFORD. Then we should get started. 'Cause I'm going to have practice in the morning.

SAUL. Okay then, big man, let's see what you got.

(**MANFORD** *takes the ball.*)

Letter 1

(**WEN CHANG** *holds a newspaper.*)

WEN CHANG. On May 7, 1989, an article ran in the San Francisco Chronicle, sports section, page twelve, regarding a supposed "rematch" between Beijing University and USF, to take place in China in one month's time. Saul Slezac, the American coach, was reported to have said –

(**SAUL** *appears.*)

SAUL. "I brought basketball to China, I taught Beijing the game. My visit changed everything, and now I'm ready for a rematch."

WEN CHANG. The number of inaccuracies in that statement is staggering. To use an ancient Chinese phrase: "What absolute bullshit." I will demonstrate.

SAUL. "I brought basketball to China, I taught Beijing the game."

WEN CHANG. Correction! China has always had basketball. It was the only western sport never banned by the party. On the grounds that it taught Communist ideals and that Mao was a big big fan.

SAUL. "And now I'm ready for a rematch."

WEN CHANG. His team had never faced mine. In his first visit, he came alone, as our guest.

(**SAUL** *disappears.*)

In fact, even the image that ran with the article?

[*Projection: An image of a crowd of Chinese people headed into a basketball game.*]

This is the original image published in the People's Daily.

[*Projection: The image cropped into the photo of Saul and Wen Chang in 1971. The handshake.*]

And THIS is the image that the San Francisco paper ran with the article, eighteen years later, re-centering the photograph on the coaches. But perhaps that is fitting, as this is the story not of the team, but the coaches. Not of those who run, but those who stand still.

(Beat.)

He did get one thing right. His visit, that photo? It did change everything.

But where to begin?

Where does anyone begin?

"It was the best of times, it was the worst of times."

It was summer 1971.

Eighteen years ago.

The height of the Cultural Revolution.

I was twenty-five, I was low-level, bottom of the barrel. I was no one.

I was laboring in Fuzhou, being rehabilitated by the Communist Party.

So when I was suddenly brought back to Beijing for the first time in five years, I figured it was the end of my story. But in reality it was the beginning.

The wheel had turned and the so-called "ping-pong diplomacy" had made us and the Americans friends again, or at least uneasy acquaintances.

The party had sought out an instructor who could teach us the American version of the game: the assistant coach at the University of San Francisco, a highly-rated, very prestigious program. And I was to be his translator. Not because I knew the game in the slightest but because after all this time, my English was still the best.

Despite myself, I was strangely excited to meet one of America's finest.

But then I saw him.

*(A younger, hairier **SAUL** appears, scratches himself.)*

SAUL. Holy mother of fuck.

WEN CHANG. His English was so bad!

SAUL. The fuck you're doing out there?!

WEN CHANG. Every single word out of his mouth, I had to go home and look up.

SAUL. Bitch pussy please.

WEN CHANG. But the dictionary it did not help!

SAUL. You show that shit! You show that shit!

WEN CHANG. In all my years studying English, never had I encountered someone who spoke the language with such blatant disregard.

SAUL. Shit and cock and balls and fuck.

WEN CHANG. Still, it was so exciting! They put me in charge of the foreigner for the length of his stay.

SAUL. Zone defense!

WEN CHANG. They wanted me to keep notes for the cultural ministry to review.

SAUL. Let's go, John, Paul, George! They say you want a revolution? Well, let's see it, Ringo!

WEN CHANG. I could not report what he was saying to the party! I could not tell them he was saying THAT.

SAUL. *Ich bin ein Beijinger*, Eleanor Rigby!

WEN CHANG. I did not even know what that meant! But I was the translator. What could I do?

SAUL. Murder that ball! Get it, get it.

WEN CHANG. I was as you say, between a rock and something else that is also hard.

SAUL. Suicides.

WEN CHANG. I did not understand.

SAUL. Eight reps, let's go!

WEN CHANG. I thought he was crazy.

SAUL. You hear what I said?

WEN CHANG. You want them to kill themselves?

SAUL. I want them to show some goddamn hustle.

WEN CHANG. These were young men who had barely escaped the countryside, who had survived the past decade by keeping their heads down, their knees bent, and their eyes on the ground in front of them. Young men who were, by necessity, unextraordinary. So things like –

SAUL. Suicides.

WEN CHANG. I could not tell them that. I had to think of something else.

> *(Beat.)*

Run back and forth so hard you think your heart will explode.

SAUL. Nice, nice.

WEN CHANG. He liked that.

SAUL. Full-court press.

WEN CHANG. Press yourself towards your opponent throughout the entire court.

SAUL. Pick up the pace. Pick it up.

WEN CHANG. Run as if you must pick up all the pages of the Little Red Book.

SAUL. Drive it to the hole!

WEN CHANG. Tractor into the pothole!

SAUL. Dunk that shit!

WEN CHANG. Turd in the well!

SAUL. Protect the rock!

WEN CHANG. *(Big gesture.)* COVER YOUR PENIS!

> *(Beat. Off* **SAUL***'s expression:)*

No?

SAUL. No.

WEN CHANG. There were some phrases I never did get.

SAUL. What're they doing out there?!

WEN CHANG. They are playing the basketball.

SAUL. That's not basketball.

WEN CHANG. Is the equipment incorrect?

SAUL. They keep passing. You can't win, you keep passing like that.

WEN CHANG. But isn't passing an essential part of the game?

SAUL. But it's not the whole game. TAKE A SHOT! What's wrong with them?

> *(Beat.)*

WEN CHANG. They do not want to miss.

SAUL. Sooner or later, we all miss.

WEN CHANG. But they do not want to choose to throw and then miss.

> *(Beat.)*

Make them all throw.

SAUL. What?

WEN CHANG. Make them take turns. Give them no choice. Then they will throw into your basket.

SAUL. Who're you again?

WEN CHANG. I was no one. I was nothing.

SAUL. So tell me, Sparky –

WEN CHANG. Wen Chang.

SAUL. Yeah, what's the deal with the team?

WEN CHANG. They are Olympic-caliber athletes.

SAUL. They're like chest height.

WEN CHANG. They were handpicked specifically for their fitness. The best in ping-pong, track and field, gymnastics –

SAUL. For a basketball team?

WEN CHANG. Since the most important things are speed and hand-eye coordination.

SAUL. If you're six feet tall!

WEN CHANG. They were supposed to be tall?

SAUL. YES. ALWAYS. Speed, accuracy, and HEIGHT. That's what you need.

WEN CHANG. And if you are someone who has none of that?

SAUL. Well, if you're not the bigger man, then you've got to BE the bigger man. Use every last inch you got.

WEN CHANG. I was very, very interested.

SAUL. I can teach you how to use the full dick.

WEN CHANG. That I did not write down.

SAUL. And if you don't got the goods, then you gotta go into the forest and cut yourself down some tall trees. You play out there, it's war. You gotta have balls. Cojones.

WEN CHANG. Testicles?

SAUL. You get in their heads, you fuck their shit up.

WEN CHANG. You copulate on their feces?!

SAUL. No! No! That's not it. Why would you say that?

WEN CHANG. That is what you just said.

SAUL. No. You insult them.

WEN CHANG. That does not seem very sportsmanlike.

SAUL. It's part of the game, it's how you show your opponents respect.

WEN CHANG. By insulting them?

SAUL. Because you believe they are a threat.

WEN CHANG. How is this useful?

SAUL. Okay, so I'm over here, I'm taking a free throw. And you: what're you doing?

WEN CHANG. I am waiting to get the ball back.

SAUL. No! Don't do that.

WEN CHANG. It is not my turn.

SAUL. It is always your turn. Every time you are on that court, it is always your turn.

WEN CHANG. It was such an American way of thinking.

SAUL. You never want to wait for someone to give you your turn back. Never wait for someone to give you what should be yours.

WEN CHANG. I had been waiting for things my whole life.

SAUL. If someone is taking a free throw, that's an opportunity for you to get the ball back.

WEN CHANG. But it is their free throw.

SAUL. Just 'cause it's a free throw doesn't make it free.

WEN CHANG. I still do not understand.

SAUL. Okay. Here. You got the ball, you're taking a free throw. No, go. Throw.

> (**WEN CHANG** *takes the ball, gets ready to shoot.*)

Cockshit!

WEN CHANG. What?

SAUL. No, no, no, go. Sorry. Try again.

WEN CHANG. All right.

> (**WEN CHANG** *tries again.*)

SAUL. THE FUCK IS THAT?!

WEN CHANG. Where?

SAUL. Sorry. Bird. Just a bird.

WEN CHANG. I fear you are distracting me.

SAUL. Exactly! That's exactly what you want to do.

WEN CHANG. Americans do that?

SAUL. We'll do it even when you're not shooting.

WEN CHANG. You said to respect the game.

SAUL. You respect the game by playing as hard as you can. They shove, you shove right back, you cocksucking chink-eyed commie red motherfucker.

WEN CHANG. Excuse me?

SAUL. For example.

WEN CHANG. Oh.

SAUL. Your turn.

WEN CHANG. Me?

SAUL. Yes! Go! Say something.

WEN CHANG. You, play terrible basketball.

SAUL. You gotta be more specific.

WEN CHANG. Because you play like a drunken Mongolian?

SAUL. And...?

WEN CHANG. You are an instrument of a capitalist state!

SAUL. Yeah!

WEN CHANG. You are not well-liked within the party!

SAUL. No, I am not!

WEN CHANG. And your parents gave up their first child because she was a girl and a cripple when they should have given up you!

SAUL. AND WHY IS THAT?

WEN CHANG. Because you are a terrible basketball player!

SAUL. AND WHERE CAN THEY STICK IT?

WEN CHANG. IN THE OVEN!

SAUL. NO!

WEN CHANG. IN A BOX!

SAUL. ALSO WRONG!

WEN CHANG. SOMEWHERE INSULTING!

SAUL. IN THEIR ASS!

WEN CHANG. WHY WOULD THEY DO THAT?!

SAUL. AND WHAT ELSE DO WE SAY?

WEN CHANG. WE SAY THEIR FATHER WAS A CAPITALIST ROADER AND THEIR MOTHER DIED DURING THE GREAT LEAP FORWARD!

SAUL. USA! USA!

WEN CHANG. *(Quietly.)* USA? USA

    (Beat.)

Some things I engaged in only for the good of the party. My superiors would understand, so I hoped.

SAUL. I'll show you one more play. It's a new one I've been cooking up.

WEN CHANG. Coach Saul –

SAUL. You don't even have to move.

WEN CHANG. How is that?

SAUL. Okay, so you and me, we're on the same team. I'm the brains, you're the big.

WEN CHANG. I am most assuredly not.

SAUL. You and me, top of the key, I got the ball, you're my bodyguard. You set a screen, I run my guy into you, and now they're confused. Who're they gonna cover?

WEN CHANG. I do not know.

SAUL. Exactly!

They cover me, I pass to you, you dunk it. BOOM.

They leave me alone, I stick it. BOOM.

Easy play either way.

WEN CHANG. I just stand there?

SAUL. You "screen."

WEN CHANG. I "screen."

SAUL. You great-wall it, yeah!

WEN CHANG. *(Joke.)* And fortify my borders against thirteenth-century nomadic invaders!

(No laugh.)

And what do you call this new play?

SAUL. The "pick and stick it."

WEN CHANG. The "pick and stick it"...?

SAUL. Big guy sets the pick, then rolls past the defender, and the little guy either dumps it to the big or sticks it in the basket.

WEN CHANG. Wouldn't it make more sense to call it a "pick and roll"?

SAUL. Nah, the "pick and stick it," it's catchier. "Pick and roll," it'll never catch on.

WEN CHANG. *(To audience.)* One month is what I told myself, I would organize my notes, I would arrange an exhibition game – five on five of our top players – and I would show the people what the American had taught us. But just before the game –

SAUL. Wen Chang?

WEN CHANG. Yes, Coach Saul?

SAUL. One last piece of advice.

WEN CHANG. Yes?

SAUL. Eighteen years, that's how long you got.

WEN CHANG. For what?

SAUL. The longest NBA careers you're gonna see are eighteen, nineteen years at best. You start at eighteen and you're lucky if you hit thirty-six and you can still run down the court without blowing your knees out. And you want to know why?

WEN CHANG. Because you Americans are always running, you can never wait your turn.

SAUL. 'Cause eighteen years and then it all starts to break down.

So you gotta ask yourself, "Who do I want to be eighteen years from now?"

WEN CHANG. A completely different person.

SAUL. That's right, Sparky.

WEN CHANG. I will pass that along, yes. I should now reserve my seat.

SAUL. Seat? You're sitting courtside, Coach.

WEN CHANG. Coach?

SAUL. Beijing University's got a full-fledged team now! Who better to lead 'em than you?

WEN CHANG. So many others.

SAUL. As soon as I hop on that plane tomorrow, they're gonna offer it to you.

WEN CHANG. ...

SAUL. You don't want it?

WEN CHANG. No. Of course, I will comply. I am very excited to comply.

SAUL. What, you don't like the game or something?

WEN CHANG. Basketball? I love it.

SAUL. Then what?

WEN CHANG. Of course I did not want it. Of course I should not take it. Of course of course of course. But little did he know, that here in China, especially in China, when someone offers you something, you must accept.

SAUL. You're gonna be someone, you know that?

WEN CHANG. Growing up, you did not want to be someone. You wanted to be the person three people behind someone. Because being someone could get you killed. But basketball changed all that.

Now there was a new China.

Now they needed someone.

And I was that someone.

(*To* **SAUL**.) I...hope I will meet your expectations.

SAUL. And when you're ready, gimme a call, I'll bring my team over, give you what for.

WEN CHANG. It may take me a long time to field those tall trees.

SAUL. How long you need?

WEN CHANG. Eighteen years?

SAUL. Then I'll see you in eighteen years, Sparks. We got a deal then?

WEN CHANG. I suppose we do.

SAUL. Put her there.

WEN CHANG. What?

> (*The handshake. Flashbulbs. The famous photo.* **SAUL** *poses.* **WEN CHANG** *is caught off-guard.*)

When he returned home, he was later quoted as saying, "No Chinese team will ever beat an American team, I promise you." An unfortunate statement to say the least. One that would haunt the party for years to come.

Scene

(**MANFORD** *stands on a different basketball court, an outdoor asphalt one in Chinatown. Broken backboard, no net. It is now night. He stands frozen at the free-throw line, still in his black suit. He stares at the basket, no ball in hand.* **CONNIE** *appears with a basketball, watches him for a moment. He doesn't see her.*)

CONNIE. Yo, Cousin!

MANFORD. Hi, Connie.

CONNIE. I hear you want to play.

MANFORD. No, I don't.

CONNIE. I hear you looking for a little one-on-one.

MANFORD. No, I'm not.

CONNIE. You've been out here for an hour now, dinner's cold, so what else do you want?

MANFORD. Go back inside, Con.

CONNIE. People be talking about how you're the best.

MANFORD. In Chinatown.

CONNIE. In any town.

MANFORD. That is simply not true.

CONNIE. You can be whatever you want to be.

MANFORD. Connie, that is absolutely one hundred percent completely untrue.

CONNIE. So let's see it, Lum. Let's go. Let's play the ball.

MANFORD. Basketball players don't say that.

CONNIE. Toss some balls. Win some baskets.

MANFORD. Con, you know basketball as well as I do. What're you doing?

CONNIE. I'm trying to cheer you up, Manford.

MANFORD. By letting me beat a girl at basketball?

CONNIE. You think you're gonna beat me?

(*She tries to dribble. She's not very good.*)

MANFORD. Just go inside.

CONNIE. Bottom of the fourth! Bounce pass to Lum! He takes the ball, he inserts it in the hoop, the crowd goes wild. Waaaaaaa! LUM LUM LUM LUM! The pride of Chinatown, the captain of Galileo –

MANFORD. – HIGH SCHOOL.

CONNIE. The star of this year's city finals!

MANFORD. Who lost in overtime.

CONNIE. MANFORD LUM!

MANFORD. In his last and final game. I'm graduating. High school is over. In three months, all my teammates'll be in college, and I'll be back at Sam Wo, delivering takeout for the rest of my life.

CONNIE. Playoffs're on. Come on. You may not be hungry, but I know you won't miss the playoffs.

MANFORD. I'm good.

CONNIE. It's Chicago vs. Cleveland. Bulls and Cavs. Game five. Jordan, man. Come on! The game's almost over.

MANFORD. How're they doing?

CONNIE. Come in, and find out.

MANFORD. Are they down?

Con, are the Bulls down?

CONNIE. Just this quarter.

MANFORD. Aaaaah! Why does everything have to be so fucked up all the time?!

CONNIE. The game is not over.

MANFORD. Yes, it is. Fuck.

CONNIE. Today was your mom's funeral and you're mad about the Bulls?

MANFORD. YES. Just cut the crap, Con, do it, yell at me, I know you're mad.

CONNIE. I'm not mad.

MANFORD. You should be.

CONNIE. Why?

MANFORD. I ran off. I left you and your parents at the service. Didn't even tell you why.

CONNIE. So you gonna tell me now?

MANFORD. I didn't have anything to say. She was a stranger to me, some lady from China I never knew. We barely even spoke the same language.

CONNIE. You could've learned more Chinese.

MANFORD. The only time we spent together was watching games. She knew more about the Warriors than she did about me.

CONNIE. That is not true.

MANFORD. She didn't take the time to get to know me, so I returned the favor, peaced out on HER.

CONNIE. So where did you go instead?

MANFORD. I went to shoot a hundred.

CONNIE. And how'd you do?

MANFORD. I got to ninety-nine and then I missed.

CONNIE. And who else in San Francisco can do that?

MANFORD. But if I still can't hit the one that counts?

CONNIE. Next time, Pro.

MANFORD. There is no next time. There is nothing out there for me. And nobody Chinese is ever playing pro.

CONNIE. Hey, go tell that to Beijing University.

MANFORD. What about Beijing University?

CONNIE. Only a matter of time before one of those guys makes his way over here, right?

MANFORD. Okay, some of us don't go to college and study abroad, Con, so some of us have no idea what you're talking about.

CONNIE. The farther north you go, the taller they get. And Beijing University is very very far north.

MANFORD. So their basketball team –

CONNIE. Yeah.

MANFORD. Omigod, they're giants.

CONNIE. Exactly.

MANFORD. And he has no idea.

CONNIE. Who?

MANFORD. Thank you, Con!

(**MANFORD** *tosses* **CONNIE** *the ball.*)

CONNIE. Where're you going? Don't you want to see how the game ends?

MANFORD. I already know how it's gonna go. Bet you Jordan wins it at the buzzer.

Scene

(Front door in a lousy apartment building in Oakland. As **SAUL** *goes to unlock door, takeout in hand:)*

MANFORD. Hi again.

*(***MANFORD*** stands in front of the door.)*

SAUL. Holy mother of fuck!

MANFORD. I don't think we got off on the right foot.

SAUL. What the hell, you're following me home now?

MANFORD. I'm giving you a second chance.

SAUL. You're giving ME?

MANFORD. I hit those free throws.

SAUL. You hit ninety-nine of them.

MANFORD. And who else on your team can do that?

SAUL. So you can shoot. But you talk big and you start trouble. And I sure as hell don't need that. I'm faxing them my roster first thing in the morning. And you are not on it. Now get out of my way, my daughter's gonna be waiting.

MANFORD. You don't have a daughter.

SAUL. Um, I got a daughter and it's her birthday. So move.

MANFORD. Coming home late, takeout for one, shoes outside the door, all of which appear to be men's size twelve.* You don't have a daughter.

SAUL. Did I say she was inside?

MANFORD. Is there somewhere else you keep her?

(Beat.)

SAUL. She lives in Jersey with her mom.

MANFORD. Who hates your guts.

SAUL. It was an amicable divorce.

MANFORD. Then why'd your ex get all the money and full custody?

---

*Please adjust this shoe size to reflect your actor's actual measurements.

SAUL. What kind of fucking hoodoo is this?

MANFORD. You're fiftysomething, single, in a one-bedroom HERE.

SAUL. Guy can't live in Oakland?

MANFORD. Nobody white lives in this part of Oakland if they don't have to. Nobody who coaches Division One athletics lives ACROSS THE BRIDGE if they don't have to.

SAUL. Well, thank you, Columbo, but my daughter's gonna call in two minutes and I don't pick up by the fourth ring, I'm on her shitlist till she's eleven, so goodnight.

MANFORD. What do you know about Beijing?

Who are their players?

What is their game?

SAUL. I taught Beijing basketball. I CHOSE their coach.

MANFORD. So what's he like? What are his strengths? His weaknesses? Do you even know WHY out of all the teams out there, they invited you back?

SAUL. Old friends. I'm doing this as a favor for their head of athletics, my old pal Sparky.

MANFORD. Who is bringing you back because he knows he can beat you.

SAUL. No Chinese team will ever beat an American team. I promise you.

MANFORD. But how do you know for sure? Have you even seen their team?

SAUL. And how would I have done that, huh? Smoke signals?

(*From inside, a phone rings.*)

I gotta go.

MANFORD. Wait!

(*Another ring.*)

SAUL. Sorry, kid.

(**SAUL** *moves to shut the door.*)

MANFORD. They are seven feet tall.

(*Door stops.*)

SAUL. Excuse me?

MANFORD. Beijing University: they are seven feet tall.

(*Another ring.*)

Aren't you going to answer that?

(*A fourth and final ring.*)

SAUL. How do you know that?

MANFORD. My cousin did her junior year abroad. At Beijing University. She went to their games. You go, you're not facing short kids like me, it's going to be Genghis Khan and worse.

SAUL. Seven-footers? You're wrong.

MANFORD. Am I?

SAUL. You gotta be.

MANFORD. But what if I'm right? And you go halfway around the world to get your ass kicked on national television by some Chinese kids you said would never be good enough?

SAUL. It's a friendship game.

MANFORD. There is no such thing as a friendship game.

SAUL. Then why am I going?

MANFORD. So you can impress your department before they can your ass next season.

SAUL. My contract's still in negotiation.

MANFORD. You finished 8-20, your last tournament appearance was in '82. You don't win this, and they're definitely not renewing your contract and it goes to that assistant coach at Duke they've been bringing in for visits. Or am I incorrect?

SAUL. Who told you that?

MANFORD. Kovitsky's lips sink ships.

SAUL. That goddamn beanpole.

MANFORD. You take Kovitsky and their seven-footers will murder him on the inside.

SAUL. How? The Chinese don't like contact, they won't knock elbows like my guys.

MANFORD. Have you BEEN to Chinatown?

SAUL. Yes, AND I did a month in China where they were terrified of the slightest contact with me.

MANFORD. You went as their guest. You're going back as their enemy. So you need a point guard who's gonna run circles around them, force the mismatches. Someone with a good inside game. Like me.

SAUL. Is that so?

MANFORD. Run and gun: they dunk for two, we score for three. Simple math. There's more to basketball than height. You know it.

SAUL. But there is a threshold, kid. A "this tall you gotta be to ride the ride."

MANFORD. Then what about you?

SAUL. Me?

MANFORD. I looked it up: the last time USF started a point guard under six feet? It was you. Before coaching, you played for USF. So ACTUALLY GOOD point guards under six feet? Calvin Murphy, Spud Webb, Muggsy Bogues, and Saul Fucking Slezac.

SAUL. I never played in the pros.

MANFORD. But you were USF's starting point guard. You played three seasons.

SAUL. Two. I played two seasons.

MANFORD. In which you and Bill Russell and K.C. Jones won back-to-back championships. THE team of the 50s.

SAUL. But then they graduated and I injured myself senior year.

MANFORD. But still your stats, you could've played for the NBA. You should've.

SAUL. But unless you can go back in time, unbreak my fucking ankle, then we'll never know, huh?

MANFORD. Unless...

SAUL. Unless what?

> (**MANFORD** *shrugs.*)

You cocky sonofabitch.

MANFORD. Do we have a deal?

SAUL. Why you keep pounding my ass about this game, Kato?

MANFORD. What're you talking about?

SAUL. Oh, I see what this is about. I can see it in your face.

MANFORD. What, no, how could you?

SAUL. You think a kid like you'll get more tail out there in Panda Town, huh? looking for some state-sponsored Suzie Wong.

MANFORD. No.

SAUL. Then what?

MANFORD. I want to play in the land of my people and just meet some, of those people that I, haven't yet met before, that's all. I want to, stick it to China, show them what they've been missing all these years.

> (*Beat.*)

I want everyone to know that I'm not just good for a "Chinese player."

SAUL. You get me the signatures I need, and I will take it under consideration.

> (*Beat.*)

MANFORD. See you tomorrow at seven.

SAUL. Practice starts at twelve.

MANFORD. I'll be there at seven. And you got that at Sam Wo, right?

SAUL. Panda Express was closed.

MANFORD. Don't eat the soup. I used to do delivery there. The meat's bad.

SAUL. It's veggie.

MANFORD. It's pork.

SAUL. I ordered the "veggie soup." If it was meat, wouldn't they tell me?

MANFORD. Chinese people will sometimes leave out the inconvenient details. You'll get used to it.

(**MANFORD** *disappears into the night.*)

Letter 2

WEN CHANG. At the big game of 1971, we expected perhaps a handful of our colleagues, a couple party heads to help us celebrate the American coach's last night in China, but that night everyone was there, including –

> (**SAUL** *and* **WEN CHANG** *courtside at halftime.*
> **WEN CHANG** *buried in his note-taking.*)

SAUL. Twelve o'clock.

WEN CHANG. I fear your watch is extremely off. It is roughly seven thirty-five. Seven minutes left in the halftime.

SAUL. No. Twelve o'clock, over there. The six-footer, directly across from us.

> (**WEN CHANG** *looks.*)

WEN CHANG. Oh. Her.

SAUL. Who is she?

WEN CHANG. What a question! How could I describe her, in a way that would do her justice?

SAUL. She a reporter?

WEN CHANG. She is no one. Now I have questions about this "halftime" –

SAUL. Forget that: go over, chat her up.

WEN CHANG. She would obviously not be interested in that.

SAUL. You sure? She's been to every single practice.

WEN CHANG. I invited her. She is an old classmate. I apologize if she has been a distraction. I did not think you would notice her.

SAUL. Big girl like that's hard to miss.

WEN CHANG. I had hoped she would be more discreet. She is simply here to help me interpret your instructions after practice.

SAUL. She knows basketball?

WEN CHANG. Oh yes.

SAUL. You like her game, huh?

WEN CHANG. She is the most magnificent player I have ever seen touch the balls.

SAUL. I'll bet.

WEN CHANG. Pardon?

SAUL. Go talk to her.

WEN CHANG. I should not.

SAUL. What? You already got a girlfriend or something?

WEN CHANG. Yes. That is it.

SAUL. Oh shit, you've been holding out on me, little man?

WEN CHANG. Yes. I have. That is why I cannot go and chat with her.

SAUL. And you and this OTHER girl, you've... *(Gestures.)* ...soaked that shit up.

WEN CHANG. What?

SAUL. Like you do.

WEN CHANG. I had grown up in the People's Republic of China, during the worst of the Cultural Revolution, the Great Leap Forward. If he thought I had time for anything other than trying to survive –!

SAUL. So that's a no?

WEN CHANG. No...I have obviously, soaked that shit up.

SAUL. Oh really.

WEN CHANG. Yes.

SAUL. When?

WEN CHANG. At least once prior to this.

SAUL. And how was it?

WEN CHANG. It was, good. Like how sex normally goes. Very, regular.

SAUL. And?

WEN CHANG. And...?

SAUL. I take you under my wing, I teach you the game, and you don't tell me shit?

WEN CHANG. Well, we were just, going back and forth most of the time.

SAUL. Uh-huh.

WEN CHANG. And it was the last two or three minutes that were the most intense, really.

SAUL. You hit that, huh?

WEN CHANG. I, hit that, huh.

SAUL. And?

WEN CHANG. And I was, hitting it and she was, hitting it. And me and her and then me and then her and then I was counting down, I was almost there, I had four, five seconds left, in the sex, and she is coming at me, and I am bringing it down the lane, split the post – between me and the, woman – and I see where I am going to, hit it and I just, nail it. You know?

SAUL. Pivot, switch, BOOM.

WEN CHANG. Right into the, vagina. Which is how I had the sex.

(A moment.)

What would I even say to her?

SAUL. "My name is Wen Chang. Would you like to Mao my dong?"

WEN CHANG. A Chinese person would never say that. Also that is not the correct pronunciation.

SAUL. Then tell me how you'd say it.

WEN CHANG. The halftime is almost over.

SAUL. Fuck your halftime. Tell me what you'd say instead.

WEN CHANG. "Hello. It is me, Wen Chang. Your longtime classmate. Would you like to discuss recent events with me?"

SAUL. "Fuck. Yes. FINALLY."

WEN CHANG. That is an unrealistic response.

SAUL. And that was a terrible come-on, but hey.

WEN CHANG. She is not my type.

SAUL. You can't even tell me what your type is.

WEN CHANG. But I could tell him what was not: someone who did things without asking, who opened their mouth at the first sign of misdeed, who ran into danger without careful consideration of the consequences. I lived in a world where I could not change jobs, move cities, breathe air without express permission from the party. So to be with someone like that? She was like basketball to me. Something best observed from afar.

SAUL. What's the problem?

WEN CHANG. She is, too tall for me!

SAUL. Hey, your biggest self, the full dick.

WEN CHANG. If she was interested in me, I would know. *(Thinks.)* Would I not?

SAUL. All I know is, I see her and she's looking at you.

WEN CHANG. Like she had never looked at me before.

SAUL. What do you have to lose?

WEN CHANG. Everything.

    (To audience.) And I knew, I should not. I should have stood my ground, but –

SAUL. *(Gestures.)* It is always your turn.

WEN CHANG. "It is always your turn."

        *(**WEN CHANG** begins to walk across the court.)*

Scene

(Morning. **MANFORD** *dressed for practice.* **CONNIE** *enters.)*

MANFORD. Have a good day!

CONNIE. You want a ride to school?

MANFORD. No. Thanks! Bye!

CONNIE. Or after, I could take you to Mervyn's, pick up a new tie for graduation.

MANFORD. Or YOU could take you to Mervyn's, pick it up for me.

CONNIE. Why? You have something else after school?

MANFORD. Yes.

CONNIE. What?

MANFORD. School. More school. So much school.

CONNIE. Your counselor called.

MANFORD. Yeah?

CONNIE. You weren't in class yesterday.

MANFORD. Think I was.

CONNIE. Think you weren't.

MANFORD. Or maybe you weren't.

CONNIE. They told me you stopped going three weeks ago. They said they've been calling, trying to get ahold of us, see why you've been cutting class.

MANFORD. Yes, that is correct.

CONNIE. So you lied to me.

MANFORD. I didn't lie! I just sometimes don't tell you all the truth.

CONNIE. Why have you been cutting class?

MANFORD. My mom is dead, my future is over, my "family" is you and your parents and a pull-out couch. Isn't that a good enough reason not to go to class?

CONNIE. They say you miss one more day and you're not graduating.

MANFORD. What?! No. I have to.

CONNIE. I agree.

MANFORD. Talk to them for me, Con. Get me out of it.

CONNIE. And tell them what?

MANFORD. I don't know. Say something. You're smart, you're old.

CONNIE. I'm twenty-five.

MANFORD. You're getting a master's degree in why Chinese people are sad.

CONNIE. Asian American Studies.

MANFORD. You sign things, write notes, translate for your parents all the time. SO: translate this into some way I graduate on time. They'll make an exception if you ask. Help me, Connie Fong, you are my only hope.

CONNIE. I never saw that movie.

MANFORD. But you still know what I'm talking about. Help me out and I will make some money, I will clear out of the living room. You will never have to see me again!

CONNIE. Why do you always say that?

MANFORD. That's what you want, isn't it?

CONNIE. I want you to explain where you've been going instead of school.

MANFORD. I got a job.

CONNIE. Where?

MANFORD. With the university.

CONNIE. Which university.

MANFORD. USF?

CONNIE. Doing what?

MANFORD. The only thing I'm good at.

CONNIE. Basketball?! You're skipping school for basketball?

MANFORD. I switched from school TO basketball.

CONNIE. That's not a job.

MANFORD. You don't know that.

CONNIE. No one's paying you to play basketball.

MANFORD. People pay people to play basketball.

CONNIE. People don't pay people like YOU to play basketball.

MANFORD. You said I can be whatever I want to be.

CONNIE. I was trying to be supportive!

> (**MANFORD** *takes out the newspaper, shows* **CONNIE**.)

MANFORD. I'm playing this game.

CONNIE. Beijing University vs. USF?

MANFORD. I'm leaving tomorrow.

CONNIE. No, you are not.

MANFORD. They already bought my plane ticket.

CONNIE. With everything that's going on over there? They've gotta cancel it.

MANFORD. Nope.

CONNIE. Do you even know what I am referring to when I say "everything that's going on over there"?

MANFORD. Yes! Kind of. Probably not.

CONNIE. There are protests going on over there right now. Massive, countrywide protests. My friends from Beijing are faxing me: they say the students won't end their hunger strike until Deng Xiaoping talks to them. The students are trying to overthrow their government and end Communism.

MANFORD. Isn't that good? Don't we like that? Didn't YOU say you're rooting for them?

CONNIE. From afar.

MANFORD. Well, I want to sit courtside. Witness history close-up!

CONNIE. Look at the papers: Beijing has been under martial law for weeks. The streets are filled with tanks and troops and who knows what else!

MANFORD. So?

CONNIE. What do you think will happen to you, a guest of the Communist Party, if WHEN you find yourself in the middle of a revolution?

MANFORD. The rest of the team doesn't care.

CONNIE. The rest of the team is Chinese?

MANFORD. *(Re: self.)* Chinese American.

CONNIE. I know you think China, you think "wow" and "cool" and "one billion other me's" but it's not. I went. And the Forbidden City, Great Wall? Not that great. Kind of broken, mostly stairs. You go to China, all you're going to see is what forty years in the dark does to a country. I didn't see myself there. And you won't either.

MANFORD. That's not what this is about.

CONNIE. It's one game, Manford. This is your life.

MANFORD. This one game, Con, it is my life. I have to go. I have to play in a game that matters.

CONNIE. You want to play in a game that matters? Then do it here, in front of your family.

MANFORD. "My family."

CONNIE. Yes.

MANFORD. You want to know why I'm going, Con?

(**MANFORD** *holds up the newspaper.*)

CONNIE. It's just an article for the game.

MANFORD. Look at the photo.

(**MANFORD** *exits.* **CONNIE** *looks at the newspaper again.*)

Scene

*(**SAUL** on the phone in his office.)*

SAUL. Beijing, that's right!

I don't make it back, just light a candle, say a mass, whatever you do with that new schlemiel on Sundays.

Hey, China, four whole days, anything could happen.

You know that once you signed those papers, you gave up your right to call me up out of the blue, first time in MONTHS, and hock my ass during school hours.

Oh come on, I'm just razzing you, Ames.

Don't go.

Put on Becks, okay?

I'm leaving tomorrow.

If this is my last will and testament, shouldn't I get to impart some wisdom onto my one and only?

I'm sorry about her birthday, but –

Well then, you make sure she calls me back, okay?

> *(**CONNIE** enters, stands in the doorway. **SAUL** sees her. Strange.)*

Hold on, Ames –

*(To **CONNIE**.)* Can I help you?

CONNIE. You're the coach.

SAUL. Yes.

CONNIE. Then we need to talk.

SAUL. Any interview requests can wait till I'm back from Beijing.

CONNIE. This is about Manford.

SAUL. I speak on behalf of the team. Kid's busy, he's going to China tomorrow.

CONNIE. You sure about that, Mr. Slezac?

SAUL. Uh, I gotta go, Ames.

Yeah, Beijing is calling!

And Saturday morning.

You don't have to make her watch. Just turn it on, okay?

(**SAUL** *hangs up.*)

SAUL. How the hell did you bust in here and who the hell are you?

CONNIE. I came in the players' entrance. Manford, my cousin, he taught me how to do that.

SAUL. It's the whole Charlie Chan Clan, isn't it?

CONNIE. You always forget about the players' entrance.

SAUL. We gotta get someone to lock those fucking doors.

CONNIE. How do you think you're going to take a minor to a foreign country without approval?

SAUL. He's his own man.

CONNIE. He's seventeen. He doesn't go unless I say so.

SAUL. I got a permission slip that says otherwise.

CONNIE. His mom died three weeks ago.

SAUL. It's a guy's handwriting.

CONNIE. And he doesn't have a dad.

SAUL. Shit.

CONNIE. So, to reiterate: he doesn't go unless I say so.

SAUL. You're gonna strip him of the game like that?

CONNIE. Why wouldn't I?

SAUL. 'Cause you do that, and you really don't have a clue who this kid is. He deserves this game.

CONNIE. He deserves to be safe. Manford doesn't know when to lay off, on and off the court. And that's what gets him in trouble.

SAUL. He gets hot, I know.

CONNIE. It's more than that. Manford went to Francisco Middle School, there were two ways you could walk home. The long way, through Chinatown. Or you could go on Columbus.

SAUL. ...?

CONNIE. You didn't grow up here, did you?

SAUL. Bronx.

CONNIE. Columbus Avenue, it's the border of Chinatown, the Italian kids, it's their turf. You walk on Columbus?

You're asking for it. It's just a fact. And every day, Manford would walk home on Columbus. So every day, he'd get jumped. Or close to it.

"Go the other way," that's what I told him.

"Can't."

"Why not?"

"That's my walk. I stop walking that way, I never get that space back."

SAUL. He's right.

CONNIE. He doesn't know when to stop. So he needs someone who's going to do it for him. And if that's not you, I need to know.

SAUL. You think I won't take care of him?

CONNIE. I think you will do whatever it takes to win this game.

SAUL. He's a hell of a point guard. He lights up my team, gets them off their asses for the first time in how long? That kid does not quit. Why would I not protect a weapon like that?

CONNIE. He is not a weapon. He is not an object. He is my cousin. So convince me that you care about him and those other players for more than just the forty-something minutes they're on that court.

SAUL. I care about my guys.

CONNIE. Always?

SAUL. It is the one thing I am actually good at.

I have watched them grow up, graduate.

I have spent more time with my players than I ever will with my own daughter.

I don't take care of my guys and who else do I have?

(Beat.)

CONNIE. Okay. That's all I wanted to know.

*(**CONNIE** hands **SAUL** a piece of paper.)*

SAUL. What is this?

CONNIE. It's a list of everyone working at the American embassy. You know them.

SAUL. I don't.

CONNIE. Well, you get in trouble, you say you do. In fact, first thing when you get to China, before you do anything else, go to the embassy, register with them. Tell them you've arrived.

SAUL. They know we're coming.

CONNIE. Make SURE they know.

>   *(Beat.)*

And see if you can get him to lay off the inside shots. He goes inside, runs right into traffic for the layup without waiting for a pass or a screen or shit.

>   **(CONNIE** *turns to go.* **SAUL** *holds out the permission slip.)*

SAUL. Before you go, can I get your John Hancock on this permission slip?

CONNIE. Nah. He's his own man.

SAUL. You're his cousin. Next of kin.

CONNIE. We're not actually related. He's not my real cousin. My dad's the super in our building. Manford's mom worked nights, as a security guard. So we'd have him over for dinner. Chinese people're weird like that.

>   *(MANFORD enters.)*

MANFORD. Con? What're you doing here?

CONNIE. I came to wish you luck. You're going to China.

MANFORD. Don't play me, Con.

CONNIE. I'll call the school. You have to go. I see that now.

SAUL. I'll bring him back to you in one piece.

CONNIE. You promise?

SAUL. It's China, four days, what could happen?

>   *(The sound of a plane taking off into the sky.)*

Intermission

Scene

(Beijing, June 1, 1989. Heat wave, everything is sticky, uncomfortable, ready to pop. The team sits in an un-air-conditioned bus. The smell of dissent and mutiny in the air. **SAUL** *is sweating like a pig. Maybe he eats a red bean popsicle.)*

SAUL. All right, you masturbating horsefuckers:

I know you're tired.

I know you're still jet-lagged from last night.

I know you'd rather be jerking off into a nice hot bowl of noodles than sitting in traffic this early in the morning.

But before I let you off this bus into first practice, I got a whole spiel the State Department wants me to give you – some Mao Ze Don'ts if you will! – because they think you idiots can't steer clear of trouble for four whole days in Beijing.

But rather than read it to you verbatim, I am going to put this into language you will hopefully understand.

*(**SAUL** holds up a Chinese newspaper.)*

This is the People's Daily.

The official newspaper of China.

This is what Deng Xiao Fucking Ping's got one billion Cabbage Patch Kids reading every day.

THIS is what he wants his country to be seeing.

And the front page here, what do you see?

*(**SAUL** holds up the newspaper.)*

"Mickey Gorbachev." YES. "The guy with the period stain on his forehead," correct.

Also known as general secretary for the USSR, waving bye-bye after his long-awaited commie gangbang with Deng Xiao Fucking Ping.

And BECAUSE Soviet menstrual face was just in town, we are surrounded by all the biggies: CBS, BBC, CNN, the whole mishpucha. Which means any jerk-offs you commit here will be beamed back home to your nanas in Dolby surround sound.

Because on the other side?

US. That's right.

The American basketball team which is DELIGHTED to be here at the invitation of Deng Xiao Fucking PING-PONG PING.

What do you not see?

Blockades. Burning trucks. Hunger strikers in Kamikaze headbands.

All that stuff going on out there? We don't care!

The students want to civil war and the party wants to let 'em?

That's not our concern.

Our concern is Peking duck and golf claps.

Our concern is Ling Ling and Sing Sing.

Our concern is winning this game.

Because while we are here, we are here as diplomats.

What does that mean?

No, wrong! That's illegal. We do not do that.

Nor does it mean we have diplomatic immunity.

Actually, here!

    (SAUL tosses the newspaper aside.)

You know Nike? You know the slogan?

"Just Do It"?

For the next four days: "Just Don't."

They put you on a bus?

Stay on the bus.

They stick you in a hotel?

Stay in the hotel.

Some student wants to practice their English on you? You say "*no bueno.*"

You so much as scratch 'n sniff the wrong cock and I will hit you so hard with suicides once we get back in the fall.

"IF I'm back in the fall?"

Oh that's nice, Wanamaker, that's real nice.

"HOW will I know you are fucking it up for all of us?"

Because the Chinese will tell me. They are the country that brought us spaghetti, they built the Great Wall, they came up with pandas, they can do anything.

Trust me: I was here in '71, I know the drill. As soon as we start first practice, we will be tailed by every Tom, Dick, and Hare Krishna within earshot.

As long as you are wearing those jerseys, you represent us. You represent America. You do something, and everyone will know.

Is that clear?

Do we need to translate that for you?

Do we need to get Lum up here to make sure all that gets absorbed?

Lum?

Where's Lum?

(A moment while they look for him.)

Shit.

Scene

(**MANFORD** *in Tiananmen Square, wearing his basketball jersey, surrounded by thousands of Chinese student protestors in white headbands. He's lost.*)

MANFORD. Excuse me, I'm looking for a –

Oh, no, sorry, I don't speak –

English? Does anyone –

(*Someone says something in English.*)

Yes, basketball!

I'm here for basketball.

America, yes.

USA

USA!

(*A chant of "USA" begins to sweep the square.* **MANFORD** *gets into it.*)

Yeah! USA! USA!

(**MANFORD** *stands frozen in his USF basketball jersey.*)

(**WEN CHANG** *appears in a different space, picks up a fax printout. The slightest realization before he collects himself.*)

Scene

(**SAUL** *and* **WEN CHANG** *in Wen Chang's fifteenth-floor apartment overlooking Tiananmen Square. Outside, sounds of the protest. Everything is just a little too sparse, too small for* **SAUL**, *who fans himself incessantly.*)

SAUL. Hot.

WEN CHANG. Yes.

SAUL. So fucking hot.

WEN CHANG. Welcome to June in Beijing.

(**WEN CHANG** *pours* **SAUL** *some tea.*)

SAUL. What is this?

WEN CHANG. Tea.

SAUL. Hot tea.

WEN CHANG. Yes. You would care for something else?

SAUL. No, tea. Why not.

(*They sip hot tea.*)

WEN CHANG. Please tell me if it is not strong enough. I still save my tea leaves. Even now, when my cupboard is stocked with plenty, I cannot bring myself to throw them out.

(**SAUL** *gestures to the A/C unit.*)

SAUL. The A/C work?

WEN CHANG. They recently installed it. It is top of the line: Toshiba.

SAUL. "Toshiba."

WEN CHANG. Yes. The cooling unit is Toshiba and the fax machine is Sony.

SAUL. Look at you: buying Japanese now.

WEN CHANG. Our memories are as conveniently short as they need to be.

SAUL. Never thought I'd see THAT day.

WEN CHANG. Much has changed, my friend.

SAUL. So should we let her rip?

WEN CHANG. What?

SAUL. See if the Japanese finally did you a solid.

WEN CHANG. Oh, I do not care for air conditioning.

SAUL. ...Oh.

WEN CHANG. An open window is still good enough for me.

SAUL. Right.

WEN CHANG. But as I recall, your constitution was not as hardy.

> (**WEN CHANG** *turns on the A/C unit.* **SAUL** *melts.*)

SAUL. Ahhhh!

WEN CHANG. Eighteen years and you have not changed.

> (**SAUL** *leans right over the A/C unit in the window, getting whatever relief he can.*)

Enjoying the view?

SAUL. Look at that oceanfront property!

WEN CHANG. Beijing is landlocked. That is Tiananmen Square down there.

SAUL. I know! Impressive! Look at you, big macher!

WEN CHANG. Your hotel room also looks out onto Chang'an Avenue.

SAUL. But nothing like this! I heard you had a million marchers down there.

WEN CHANG. That was one month ago. Now, the crowds are thinning out. The protests will be forgotten. And Beijing will have other things to talk about. Like my upcoming win.

SAUL. Against who?

WEN CHANG. Were you not informed of your upcoming loss?

SAUL. You sure about that? 'Cause my daughter, she tells me we're gonna wipe the floor with you.

WEN CHANG. Then it will be a terrible shame when you encounter my tall trees.

SAUL. You mean those seven-foot bamboo poles?

WEN CHANG. New additions to the team. It was your suggestion.

SAUL. Didn't realize they came that tall around here. You could've warned me.

WEN CHANG. Eighteen years, you could not have assumed that my team would look the same.

SAUL. Why not? I mean, you do.

WEN CHANG. Do I?

SAUL. Don't lord it over me. Eighteen years, and you still look the same! I look like shit.

WEN CHANG. That is true, yes.

SAUL. How is that?

WEN CHANG. You Americans wear all your hardships on the outside.

SAUL. And where do you wear yours?

WEN CHANG. I keep mine where no one can see.

SAUL. So out with it. What is it you dragged my ass up all those stairs for?

WEN CHANG. We have not had the opportunity to talk since you landed.

SAUL. And?

WEN CHANG. Your point guard.

SAUL. Manford?

WEN CHANG. He cannot play in tomorrow's game.

SAUL. Why not?

WEN CHANG. You did not submit his documentation on time.

SAUL. State Department cleared him, YOUR department cleared him.

WEN CHANG. You brought ten men. You are under no obligation to play all of them.

SAUL. He's my point guard.

WEN CHANG. And a month ago, he was not even on your team, yes?

SAUL. What is this?

WEN CHANG. I am providing you with a simple exit.

SAUL. This is an easy out? From what?

> (**WEN CHANG** *takes the fax printout, shows it to* **SAUL.**)

WEN CHANG. I was faxed this last evening.

SAUL. What is it?

WEN CHANG. A photograph of your player, in Tiananmen Square.

> (**SAUL** *squints at the fax printout.*)

SAUL. How do you even know that's him?

WEN CHANG. He is wearing his jersey.

SAUL. He got lost.

WEN CHANG. In Tiananmen Square.

SAUL. Maybe he thought it was a Live Aid concert. "Heal the world."

WEN CHANG. He was leading students in an obscene chant.

SAUL. What'd he say?

WEN CHANG. "USA USA"

SAUL. Oh come ON, that's every titty bar in America.

WEN CHANG. Surrounded by student protestors in white headbands. It was a clear political protest. A declaration of war.

SAUL. War?! Are you crazy?

WEN CHANG. Less than twenty-four hours on Chinese soil and this is what he does. How could you do this to me?

SAUL. Me?!

WEN CHANG. I invited your university. I publicized this match. I have organized every aspect of this game. If one of your players should disobey you further, who do you think they will hold responsible?

SAUL. As head honcho, don't you say what goes?

WEN CHANG. My sphere of influence is limited to athletics only. The party has been on edge ever since the protests began. They do not need an additional concern at the moment.

SAUL. Sparks, come on: it's a friendship game.

WEN CHANG. Do you really think that?

SAUL. What else are we here for?

WEN CHANG. You were brought here because the party does not forget a slight.

SAUL. What slight?

WEN CHANG. "No Chinese team will ever beat an American team, I promise you."

SAUL. Thought you said your memories are conveniently short.

WEN CHANG. Some things are never forgotten.

SAUL. He's a stupid American.

WEN CHANG. He is Chinese. So he should not be that dumb, yes?

SAUL. So you're penalizing him for his race?

WEN CHANG. I am penalizing him for his actions.

SAUL. 'Cause of what he looks like, you're taking out my best player?

WEN CHANG. HE'S your best player?

SAUL. Oh, don't play dumb with me. I see what this is. You think you can cheat your way to a win?

WEN CHANG. My team will most assuredly beat you, Saul.

SAUL. You pull him and I will take this to the papers.

WEN CHANG. Your Mandarin was nonexistent as I recall.

SAUL. But the crowd of folks in my lobby, the Great Wall Hotel, the swanky shit you put us up in? Swarming SWEATING SEETHING with reporters, AP, Reuters, BBC, all coming to the game tomorrow.

(*Beat.*)

New York Times.

WEN CHANG. You do not pull him and I will cancel the game.

SAUL. You think I'd cut this kid just 'cause you say so? You think I need this that much?

WEN CHANG. You came here, June in Beijing, 10,000 kilometers, and fifteen flights of stairs. That is how much you need this.

SAUL. ...

WEN CHANG. You are 8-20.

You are financially underwater.

You are the punch line of the West Coast Conference.

You are an onlooker to your own life.

Whereas, I coach the best team in China.

I don't need this. You do.

SAUL. You're not cancelling it. Lose face like that? Ruin everything you hold dear?

WEN CHANG. You have no idea what I hold dear.

(*Beat.*)

You will fax me your starting lineup by midnight tonight. If he is on it, you know what I will do.

SAUL. I gave you this job. I made you into someone.

WEN CHANG. But you never asked me if I wanted to be that someone.

SAUL. 'Cause I didn't have to! 'Cause I could read it on your face.

WEN CHANG. And now I, too, can make decisions on your behalf.

(*Beat.*)

You think you can come in and move through this country as if everything will not be reported back to Deng Xiao Fucking Ping-Pong Ping?

(*Beat.*)

SAUL. Holy shit.

WEN CHANG. I leave it up to you.

(**WEN CHANG** *recedes from view.*)

Scene

(Hallway of the Great Wall Hotel. **MANFORD** *stands in the doorway of his room.* **SAUL** *stands in the hall. Late at night. Mid-conversation:)*

MANFORD. There's gotta be another way.

SAUL. I'm sorry, kid.

MANFORD. Put me on the bench, I don't have to start. I can be your sixth man, your benchwarmer, your something, your anything.

SAUL. I can't.

MANFORD. Why are you punishing me? 'Cause I skipped first practice?

SAUL. What were you doing in Tiananmen Square?

MANFORD. I don't know, I got lost. It wasn't me!

SAUL. You sure about that?

*(***SAUL** *takes out the xerox of Manford in Tiananmen Square.)*

First day: what did I tell you guys on the bus about not fucking with those student protestors?

MANFORD. I don't know because I was / not on that bus!

SAUL. "Not on that bus." Right.

MANFORD. This isn't what you think it is.

SAUL. Then tell me what this is, let me help. You got in over your head? That's okay, but you gotta be straight with me. You gotta help me understand.

MANFORD. *(Shrugs.)* My bad.

SAUL. Then I can't play you.

MANFORD. I have been waiting for this my whole life.

SAUL. There will be other games.

MANFORD. Not like this.

SAUL. It's too late, Manford. Game's tomorrow.

MANFORD. You promised me.

SAUL. You ran off. You did this to yourself. Can't take the risk.

MANFORD. And that's how you end up 8-20. That's how you end up some failed point guard who never played pro.

SAUL. No, 'cause I was stupid like you.

MANFORD. 'Cause you never took a chance.

SAUL. Do you want to know how I ended my career?

MANFORD. You got injured.

SAUL. I injured myself.

MANFORD. That is the exact same thing.

SAUL. First game of the season, my senior year, I roll my ankle in warm-ups. Coach asks me how I'm doing, and I know I'm no good for the game, but fuck it, there's a scout, I have to. This is my big chance. So I go in and not two minutes into the game? I'm out for the rest of the season, the rest of my career: 'cause I was too stupid to wait.

> *(Beat.)*

A coach who cared less would probably let you play. But to me, you guys are family.

MANFORD. Funny, that a guy who can't even get on the phone with his own daughter considers me family.

SAUL. You really have a death wish, don't you?

MANFORD. At least I know how to pick up when my family calls.

SAUL. Your family? You mean your neighbors? The people who can't wait till you hit eighteen so they can dump your ass without the guilt trip?

> *(Beat.)*

I'm sorry, I shouldn't have said that.

And to answer your question, it happened 'cause I was too in love with the game to see anything else.

'Cause I thought my family would always be there for me once the season was over, whenever I bothered to finally come home, conquering hero.

I let the game get bigger than the rest of my life.

  (Beat.)

MANFORD. *(Re: xerox.)* Who gave you this?

SAUL. Doesn't matter.

MANFORD. It was him, wasn't it?

SAUL. You can watch the game tomorrow from the hotel.

  *(**SAUL** leaves.)*

Scene

*(Wen Chang's apartment once again, early morning. The lights flick on. **MANFORD** in the center of the apartment. **WEN CHANG** sees him.)*

MANFORD. Morning.

WEN CHANG. How did you get in here?

MANFORD. Back door, service entrance.

WEN CHANG. I am sorry, I do not believe I know you, so I will have to ask you to go.

MANFORD. You took me out of the game, you know who I am.

WEN CHANG. Please go. Or I will call security.

*(**WEN CHANG** goes to his phone.)*

MANFORD. No, you won't.

WEN CHANG. You have broken curfew, you have invaded my space. You think I will not report you?

MANFORD. Then go ahead.

*(**WEN CHANG** puts down the phone.)*

WEN CHANG. How did you find me?

MANFORD. I heard you had a view of Tiananmen Square. The students pointed you out from the street.

WEN CHANG. What do you want?

*(**MANFORD** takes out the American newspaper.)*

"Beijing University vs. USF."

MANFORD. The other side of the page, bottom right.

(Beat.)

The obituaries.

*(**WEN CHANG** sees the obituary.)*

WEN CHANG. Why are you showing me this?

MANFORD. Growing up, I only knew three things about my mom.

She was born in China.

She followed the Warriors.

And the only photo she ever kept was of two men shaking hands at a basketball game.

I was eight when I found it.

WEN CHANG. You are very good at finding what does not want to be found.

MANFORD. How'd you know my mom?

WEN CHANG. She never told you?

MANFORD. Her English was shit.

WEN CHANG. You never learned Chinese?

MANFORD. She didn't teach me. Said she didn't want me getting confused.

WEN CHANG. Your mother and I were, classmates. Enrolled, taken, into the same special English learning program.

MANFORD. But you speak it real good.

WEN CHANG. Really well, yes. I have always been a very diligent student. The qualifying exam I took as a young child was purposely long, four hours. I was the only one patient enough to sit through the whole thing.

MANFORD. But even your accent.

WEN CHANG. I had a literary recording for reference. I listened to it over and over to master the correct pronunciations. Today you would call it a "book on tape."

MANFORD. What was the book?

WEN CHANG. "It was the best of times, it was the worst of times."

MANFORD. I don't read books.

WEN CHANG. It is a story about a man who sacrifices everything for the woman he loves. Such an un-Chinese sentiment. The record was made in London, by a company called "Manford." I always liked the name, it felt like the name of someone very far away from myself.

MANFORD. So what about my mom?

WEN CHANG. Your mother? She did not want to study what they gave her. I had to help her with all her exams. She was always off playing the basketball.

MANFORD. My mom never played basketball.

WEN CHANG. Manford, she was six foot two.

MANFORD. Oh.

WEN CHANG. You never saw her play?

MANFORD. No.

WEN CHANG. Then you missed out on a legend. Her feet always flying, her mouth always running. I would give anything to see her play again.

MANFORD. Put me back in the game.

WEN CHANG. That decision is up to your coach, not me.

MANFORD. Can't you do whatever you want?

WEN CHANG. Not even Deng Xiaoping can do that.

MANFORD. But isn't he like, the president?

WEN CHANG. The chairman remembers a time when he was not. When he was at the bottom of the wheel. And that fear of going back is something you never forget.

MANFORD. The students have no fear.

WEN CHANG. Because they came of age in a China without fear. The only reason those students are not yet detained or worse? Because they are the children of party officials, who think they can do as they please.

MANFORD. They aren't afraid to die.

WEN CHANG. They are only afraid to die with no one watching. Why do you think they write so many of their signs in English? So that the world may see them.

MANFORD. The signs are for him. They just wanna talk.

WEN CHANG. Even that is still too large a request.

MANFORD. Let me play –

WEN CHANG. And in the course of that game, if anyone should discover what you are?

MANFORD. And what am I?

WEN CHANG. A rabble-rouser.

MANFORD. And what else?

WEN CHANG. A fool.

MANFORD. And what else?

WEN CHANG. An arrogant overseas Chinese who has come here for mysterious purposes.

MANFORD. You know why I'm here.

WEN CHANG. I can only speculate.

MANFORD. Tell me what I am to you, and after today, you will never see me again.

WEN CHANG. ...

MANFORD. Well?

WEN CHANG. You are, I hear –

MANFORD. Yes?

WEN CHANG. – An extraordinary player. You are...so unlike me.

MANFORD. And you want to know who you are?

WEN CHANG. I am well aware.

MANFORD. No one. You are no one. You are someone who's been standing still his whole life.

WEN CHANG. That is correct.

>   (**MANFORD** *exits, leaving the newspaper in* **WEN CHANG***'s lap.*)

Letter 3

WEN CHANG. I realize I write this letter as if incidents such
   as the Cultural Revolution hold any meaning for you,
   when in fact they may not.
   So briefly: In our attempt to prove our loyalty to the
   party and its ideals of Communism, children betrayed
   parents, friends irrevocably split. And if your lover
   writes an inflammatory pamphlet criticizing the party
   and is scheduled to be sent down to hard labor in the
   countryside, then what can you do but break off the
   attachment as soon as possible?
   But your mother failed to see it in a similar light.
   The last time I saw her was on the court.

> *(The sound of someone practicing basketball
> late at night.)*

By this time, her relocation to Hebei was imminent.
But she would not stand for this.
Instead, she told me, she was pregnant.
She was leaving.
And, most absurdly, would I accompany her to the
United States?
Ridiculous.
But I allowed myself one night to consider the
possibility, to dream of it.

> *(The practice stops.)*

Please do not stop.
I was just admiring.

> *(Practice begins again.)*

I have considered your request.
But –
(To audience.) What could I say? How could I put it?
I could not go back to the bottom.
I could not go back to that.
So –

(To her.) I am busy at the moment.

But I encourage you to do what you must.

And perhaps one day I will see you play again –

(The basketball slams against the floor.)

Will you listen to what I am trying to say?

(The sound of a basketball thrown against a wall. And then silence.)

What she did was impossible. 1971, we were not yet open to the West. To leave China then was absolutely unheard of. How she did it? I wish I knew. After her departure, I never heard from her again.

I was right, of course: five years later, our country opened, circumstances improved. But by that time, I was too valuable to go anywhere else.

And her absence was noted in my dossier, ensuring that I would never leave this country. Every year I applied for a visa, and every year, like the movement of a clock: denied.

I was the pick

And she was the roll

And together we could have done so much.

But she could not be patient

And I was too much so.

Scene

(Over the phone:)

MANFORD. What do I do?

CONNIE. Manford?

MANFORD. What do I do?

CONNIE. Manford, is everything okay? Where are you? I have been getting faxes every hour from my friends all over China, what is going on out there?

MANFORD. Con, this is long-distance.

CONNIE. Yes.

MANFORD. This is like five dollars a minute.

CONNIE. I know.

MANFORD. So you need to hurry up and tell me what I should do.

CONNIE. FIRST: what DID you do?

MANFORD. I saw him, Con. I saw him, and he wouldn't say it. He wouldn't even tell me what I am to him. He just took me out of the game.

CONNIE. I'm sorry for that, Manford.

MANFORD. And now the game and now I can't and now he'll never and now and now – I don't know what comes next.

   (Beat.)

Worst thing you can do to a Chinese person.

CONNIE. What? Why?

MANFORD. 'Cause Imma find him and Imma do it.

CONNIE. No, you're not.

MANFORD. You sure about that?

CONNIE. He never came, fine, he never wrote, yes, but why do you think he was never able to do those things?

MANFORD. Doesn't matter, shouldn't matter. If he wanted to be with us, he could've. He CHOSE.

CONNIE. He grew up in Communist China.

MANFORD. So did Mom. She left. She got out.

CONNIE. Your mom was the exception. She came to America at a time when NO ONE was leaving China. And that trip, Manford? It cost her, for the rest of her life.

MANFORD. If he wanted to, he would have been there.

CONNIE. And are you mad at Rick Barry?

MANFORD. The basketball player?

CONNIE. He played for the Warriors, you loved him, you worshipped him, and then in '78, he left to play for the Rockets.

MANFORD. That wasn't his fault.

CONNIE. He abandoned his team.

MANFORD. Rick Barry had no choice. He got traded. Free agency didn't start till last year. It was the system.

CONNIE. He could've protested the trade. Spoken up.

MANFORD. And get blackballed from the association? Pssh, it would've wrecked his whole career, his whole life.

CONNIE. Same with your dad.

MANFORD. And why're you bringing up Rick Barry?!

CONNIE. He used to be your favorite player.

MANFORD. My mom's. He was my MOM's favorite player.

CONNIE. No, he wasn't.

MANFORD. Then who was it?

CONNIE. Manford, your mom's favorite player was you.

MANFORD. Pshh!

CONNIE. What did she always say to you?

MANFORD. "Go outside," she said. "Go outside."

CONNIE. That was advice. For basketball.

MANFORD. Because she wanted me to get fresh air.

CONNIE. Because she wanted you to lay off the inside shots.

MANFORD. Oh.

CONNIE. You never see what's right in front of you.

MANFORD. Then why didn't you tell me?

CONNIE. I tried to. All the time.

MANFORD. Why didn't you tell me she played ball?

CONNIE. Your mom played basketball?

MANFORD. She was a legend, Con. She was six foot two!

CONNIE. So all this time. It wasn't him. It was her.

    (Beat.)

Go. Play.

MANFORD. Con, didn't you hear me earlier? I'm BANNED. They're not even gonna let me through the front door!

CONNIE. And when has that ever stopped you?

    (Beat.)

Help them, Manford Lum, you are their only hope.

MANFORD. The game's almost started.

CONNIE. So?

MANFORD. I had my chance. It's too late.

CONNIE. No, it's not. What did your mom say about every game?

MANFORD. *(Rolls eyes.)* "Every game is same thing."

CONNIE. No.

MANFORD. "Every game is same thing all over again."

CONNIE. "Every game is a second chance."

MANFORD. What?

CONNIE. "A second chance to live your life all over again." So show me she was right.

Scene

SAUL. Midday.

WEN CHANG. Day of the game.

SAUL. Hot as fuck.

WEN CHANG. June in Beijing.

SAUL. On the bus.

WEN CHANG. Riding out to the arena.

SAUL. The windows blacked out.

WEN CHANG. Discreetly curtained so that you may focus on your task ahead.

SAUL. Amid the eerie calm.

WEN CHANG. As you pass carefully through the streets of Beijing.

SAUL. Your tenth player conspicuously absent.

WEN CHANG. All for the best.

SAUL. As you reach the arena.

WEN CHANG. Already crowded with party members.

SAUL. Every Tom, Dick, and Hare Krishna.

WEN CHANG. BBC, CNN.

SAUL. Swarming SWEATING SEETHING with reporters.

WEN CHANG. Every camera is sitting courtside.

SAUL. Everyone is watching.

WEN CHANG. This is China. Everyone is always watching. They want to see the matchup.

SAUL. The toe-to-toe.

WEN CHANG. The neck-and-neck.

SAUL. One game.

WEN CHANG. Four quarters.

SAUL. A rematch eighteen years in the making.

WEN CHANG. That was never a rematch to begin with.

      (Whistle.)

SAUL. The tip-off.

WEN CHANG. The starting point.

SAUL. Get it get it.

WEN CHANG. Run him down!

SAUL. Easy play. Pick and roll. That's how we do it in the states.

WEN CHANG. Our ball.

SAUL. Be my guest.

(*Out.*) You're making it look too easy!

(*To* **WEN CHANG**.) Or you're making it look too hard.

WEN CHANG. We're nothing if not hospitable. You'd better hurry if you want to catch up.

SAUL. We scored first.

WEN CHANG. And that will be the end of your lead.

The pass.

SAUL. The flip.

WEN CHANG. The backdoor.

From now on, every point, we make you fight for.

SAUL. You murder that ball. Get it, get it!

WEN CHANG. Back and forth! Heart explode!

SAUL. Biggest self, full dick!

WEN CHANG. Press yourself!

SAUL. Let's see it, Ringo!

WEN CHANG. All the pages!

SAUL. *Ich bin ein* Eleanor Rigby!

WEN CHANG. You get every layup, every point, every –

SAUL. What was that?!

WEN CHANG. THAT was my tall trees.

SAUL. That's a FOUL!

WEN CHANG. That's a score. And an easy two points.

SAUL. Fucking Chinese refs.

WEN CHANG. Administering American rules.

SAUL. You don't call that a foul?

WEN CHANG. I call that a successful drive to the basket.

SAUL. I taught you that.

WEN CHANG. And I improved upon it. What did you think this game would be?

Peking duck and golf claps?

SAUL. Genghis Khan and worse.

WEN CHANG. Chasing rebounds, making contact.

SAUL. Shit and cock and balls and fuck.

WEN CHANG. Watch your language. We're on tv, you know.

CONNIE. Back at home, every set.

SAUL. CBS.

WEN CHANG. CCTV.

CONNIE. Every house.

WEN CHANG. Every eye.

SAUL. I know she's watching.

WEN CHANG. They're always watching.

CONNIE. All crowded around our TV waiting to see what forty years in the dark does to a country.

WEN CHANG. All the time zones.

SAUL. The whole mishpucha!

I can feel her.

CONNIE. Out there in the crowd.

SAUL. Your daughter.

CONNIE. Your city.

WEN CHANG. The party.

SAUL. Your ex and that new schlemiel on Sundays.

CONNIE. Your cousin, where is he?

SAUL. And what do you not see?

WEN CHANG. What is barely heard.

CONNIE. The sound of voices, protestors?

WEN CHANG. Rabble-rousers.

CONNIE. Shouts you can make out.

WEN CHANG. Across town.

SAUL. Across an ocean.

CONNIE. You turn up the volume on the game.

WEN CHANG. And drown out their voices.

CONNIE. As score after score after score.

SAUL. *(Enraged.)* THEY dunk for two, WE score for three!

WEN CHANG. Simple math.

SAUL. Not the other way around!

CONNIE. And then second quarter.

WEN CHANG. End of the half.

CONNIE. Caught in traffic.

SAUL. What the fuck!

CONNIE. And down goes Jackson.

WEN CHANG. *(As announcer.)* Halftime! Forty-seven to twelve, Beijing.

SAUL. Help your fucking teammate off the court!

WEN CHANG. Locker room! Circle up!

SAUL. I'm gonna dispense with the inspirational spiel, gentlemen. Just don't get yourselves fucking hurt out there, okay?

WEN CHANG. Your halftime?

You say nothing.

Your players have identified the party members.

They have counted the guards.

They already know what is at stake.

(To his players.) Just see this through to the other side.

CONNIE. The buzzer sounds.

SAUL. Game resumes.

WEN CHANG. Our ball!

CONNIE. As the brutal slaughter.

WEN CHANG. Moves down the court.

SAUL. WHY ARE THEY NOT SHOWING THAT SHIT?!

CONNIE. And the injuries pile up.

Hunt!

SAUL. Can't shoot, won't shoot.

CONNIE. What're they doing out there?

SAUL. Chokes on the ball when you give it to him.

CONNIE. Fisher!

SAUL. I've seen eunuchs!

Wanamaker! Get up off the floor!

CONNIE. Injured injured always injured.

WEN CHANG. You're gonna be playing with four men in a minute.

SAUL. What else can I do about it?

CONNIE. And then out of the corner of your eye.

WEN CHANG. Out of breath.

CONNIE. Out of nowhere.

WEN CHANG. There he is.

MANFORD. Wait!

SAUL. Holy mother of fuck!

CONNIE. Your cousin.

WEN CHANG. Your rabble-rouser.

SAUL. Your cocky sonofabitch.

CONNIE. And down goes Kovitsky!

MANFORD. I'm here. I'm late.

SAUL. You're banned.

MANFORD. And yet, you look pretty happy to see me.

SAUL. How the hell did you bust in here?

CONNIE. The players' entrance!

MANFORD. Put me in.

WEN CHANG. Keep him out.

MANFORD. I will win you games.

I will score you points.

I am quick. I am relentless.

I am the most relentless person you have ever met and if you have met someone more relentless than me, tell me, tell me, tell me what I want to hear.

SAUL. And you know.

MANFORD. Just say it.

SAUL. Once you say it.

MANFORD. Say it say it say it.

SAUL. You may regret this for the rest of your life.

WEN CHANG. Saul, you would not dare.

SAUL. Get in there.

MANFORD. …

SAUL. Lum, did you hear me? Before I change my mind.

MANFORD. Yes, Coach.

>   (**MANFORD** *strips down to his uniform.*)

SAUL. Here we go.

CONNIE. There he goes.

MANFORD. Fast break.

CONNIE. Catch up.

MANFORD. Three points!

SAUL. Broke your streak.

WEN CHANG. And you know what you must do.

SAUL. Lum to Fisher to Lum to Hunt!

WEN CHANG. Give the signal.
>   End the game.
>   But then –

SAUL. He's coming, he is bringing it down the lane.

CONNIE. Split the post.

MANFORD. And you see where you're going to hit it and you
>   just.

CONNIE. Nail it.

SAUL. Pivot. Switch BOOM.

WEN CHANG. You realize.

MANFORD. "Every game is same thing."

WEN CHANG. "Every game is a second chance –"

CONNIE. "– To live your life all over again."

WEN CHANG. You know his game
>   you have seen it before.

MANFORD. On the inside.

CONNIE. Without waiting for a pass or a screen or shit.

WEN CHANG. He plays his mother's game and he doesn't
>   even know it.

You send back in your starters.

MANFORD. Bring it.

WEN CHANG. The young men you built
against the one you made.
How good is he?

SAUL. You got this!

WEN CHANG. You watch with glee, with pride, with fear.

CONNIE. As he loses them all in traffic.

SAUL. Outguns your slow-moving forest.

MANFORD. Ankle-breakers, spin moves.

CONNIE. Beat for beat, pound for pound
there is no one who can match him.

WEN CHANG. In a moment, you will end this game.
You have to.
But eighteen years, what's one moment more?

SAUL. As he plays the game of his life.

MANFORD. Seizing my biological destiny.

CONNIE. Connecting passes, finding routes.

SAUL. And you wonder who taught this kid how to play?

MANFORD. Me, myself, and I.

WEN CHANG. Someone so unlike you.

CONNIE. Everything he did, he did himself.

MANFORD. Without you over my shoulder.

WEN CHANG. Behind my back.

SAUL. Between the legs.

MANFORD. Watch me cross your mind more than I ever did
in eighteen years.

WEN CHANG. Not true.

MANFORD. Every ball.

WEN CHANG. Every minute.

CONNIE. After school.

MANFORD. Every basket.

WEN CHANG. Every moment.

CONNIE. Walking home.

MANFORD. Growing up.

WEN CHANG. In the office.

CONNIE. Crossing Columbus.

MANFORD. I was no one.

WEN CHANG. I was nothing.

CONNIE. You couldn't stop him.

MANFORD. I was rec center.

WEN CHANG. I was low-level.

MANFORD. I was food stamps.

WEN CHANG. I was bottom of the barrel.

MANFORD. Last of the pick.

WEN CHANG. Runt of the litter.

MANFORD. But I was there.

WEN CHANG. Or at least I tried to be.

MANFORD. Bullshit.

WEN CHANG. What do you want me to do about it?

MANFORD. The only thing you've ever done. I want you to stand still and watch all your mistakes come back to bite you.

SAUL. Back in it.

CONNIE. Down by twelve.

SAUL. Hit those threes.

CONNIE. Close that gap against.

SAUL. "The best team in China."

WEN CHANG. You know your players.
They will not stand for this.

CONNIE. Manford, watch out!

SAUL. Lum, lay off the inside!

WEN CHANG. They dig into him just like you have taught them to.

CONNIE. And now every play.

SAUL. Every move.

CONNIE. Is a move towards Manford. Body checks.

SAUL. Flagrant shit. Blocking, flopping.

MANFORD. "Unsportsmanlike conduct"?!

WEN CHANG. Refrain from that! Leave him be!

SAUL. But they refuse to back off.

WEN CHANG. Who ordered this?!

CONNIE. Go the other way!

MANFORD. Can't.

CONNIE. Why not?

WEN CHANG. This game? Your court?

MANFORD. I will never get that space back.

WEN CHANG. You have lost control.
Someone else is giving them orders now.
This has become much bigger than yourself.

CONNIE. As all across the city
fax machines begin to buzz with activity.

WEN CHANG. Rumors, warnings.

CONNIE. The tanks are coming back.

WEN CHANG. The army is doubling down.

CONNIE. They're going to sweep the students from the square.

WEN CHANG. And you can see how this will end.
There will be no winner in this confrontation.

CONNIE. They will all be sent back into darkness.
Giving way to a generation for whom June fourth will mean nothing.

SAUL. But for every shot he takes, every shove he clocks.

CONNIE. He comes back.

MANFORD. Stronger.

WEN CHANG. Reckless.

SAUL. Fearless.

WEN CHANG. He will not stand down.
He will not go outside.

CONNIE. And you see it spread to the rest of his team.

SAUL. Transcending sloppy fundamentals and lazy footwork.

WEN CHANG. They have spent long enough on the sidelines.

MANFORD. This is their game, too.

CONNIE. Neck-and-neck.

MANFORD. Tie it up!

SAUL. Let's go! Let's move!

CONNIE. As students begin to chant.

MANFORD. USA? USA?

CONNIE. But it's not that.

WEN CHANG. And the word.

SAUL. Like an ocean.

CONNIE. Like a wave.

MANFORD. And for the first time in your life, you understand what they are saying.

WEN CHANG. They are saying his name.

CONNIE. They're cheering for him in Chinese.

WEN CHANG. They root for themselves, against themselves, by cheering for a face that looks like theirs but not.

MANFORD. They're your crowd now.

SAUL. The noise reaches a fever pitch.

WEN CHANG. And you get a note from the party:
"End this game."
"End it now."
There is still something you can do.
To reassert yourself.
Prove your loyalty.

MANFORD. Almost there!

CONNIE. Seven seconds, final play.

SAUL. One point behind. Just one point behind.

MANFORD. Inbounds.

WEN CHANG. Man-to-man.

SAUL. No one's open!

CONNIE. And then a lane opens up.

MANFORD. On the inside.

CONNIE. His favorite shot.

MANFORD. There for the taking.

CONNIE. As the clock winds down.

SAUL. Drive it in!

WEN CHANG. Up against one of my tall trees.

MANFORD. Five foot seven against seven foot –

CONNIE. Five, four –

WEN CHANG. He will not make it.

He will not pass.

CONNIE. Three, two –

SAUL. Take your shot!

MANFORD. Square up –

CONNIE. At the buzzer!

SAUL. HOLY SHIT, LUM!

CONNIE. A shot in the face.

WEN CHANG. From one of my tall trees.

CONNIE. Manford!

SAUL. Kid, you okay?!

WEN CHANG. And the referee has no choice but to call it.

SAUL. Oh NOW we're deciding to do our jobs, are we?

CONNIE. And the thing on your screen you know to be your cousin doesn't get up.

WEN CHANG. You run to the center of the court

Before you remember

This is not your son

This is just another player

Who looks like someone you could've known.

SAUL. I got this.

WEN CHANG. You return to being an onlooker to your own life. Someone who is always watching.

(**MANFORD** *is now bleeding from the forehead.*)

SAUL. How are you doing, son?

MANFORD. Fine.

SAUL. You're gonna need stitches.

MANFORD. I'm finishing this game.

CONNIE. From the safety of thousands of miles away, you see it: security guards multiplying at their posts and party leaders disappearing through some back channel. Who doesn't stay for the end of a game?

WEN CHANG. One who already knows what will happen.

SAUL. Okay.

MANFORD. At the free-throw line.

SAUL. Here we go.

CONNIE. Two shots.

SAUL. Just like we practiced.

MANFORD. A hundred baskets.

CONNIE. All night.

MANFORD. Every night.

SAUL. And you say a mass or a prayer to whatever the hell god might be watching.

MANFORD. First shot.

CONNIE. Get it, get it.

MANFORD. Got it.

SAUL. Tie game!

CONNIE. Seventy-eight all.

WEN CHANG. As you realize: a tie. End this in a tie. For safety reasons, capacity issues. A tie will be respectable. A tie will say you have done your job. "Do your job." Stop this game, send him home, and with luck, this will be the last time you see him.
(Out.) Time out!

> (WEN CHANG *walks over to* MANFORD *at the free-throw line. He moves to end the game, and then a shift.*)

> (*He looks at* MANFORD.)

"Take your shot."

> (WEN CHANG *walks off the court, out of the building, and into the night.*)

(**MANFORD** *repositions himself at the free-throw line. He bounces the ball, shoots.*)

(*As soon as it leaves his hands, he knows what will happen.*)

(*He braces himself for the moment after.*)

(*Just before the wave hits.*)

Letter 4

(The end of a letter.)

WEN CHANG. June 5, 1989.

Today.

A day they are already learning to forget.

I have spent the past thirty-six hours in my apartment observing the square. It is early morning, and the gunfire is now only sporadic.

They are dealing with their most immediate threats.

Soon they will get to me.

They suspect, I suppose, that I will not run.

They are right.

They know where to find me.

I have lived in this same apartment for eighteen years, as long as I have been coach. And in this time, I have gone neither up nor down, never reassigned nor sent down, and I used to consider that the thing I was most proud of.

But I was wrong.

To my son:

What else do you need to know?

That I loved the game even if I never played it.

That it is possible to love something from afar.

I hope this letter gives you what you want, what I could not provide firsthand.

I cannot tell you what will happen next.

The future, frankly, terrifies me.

I do not even know if you will receive this.

But I am faxing this letter to the University of San Francisco with the hope they will pass it along to you.

And if I have done my job properly, you are on your flight now, minor injuries, back to a country that will hopefully see you for the man you are.

Either way, my story ends here.

And yours is still to begin.

(**WEN CHANG** *begins to dress for the day.*)

Today the streets are empty, and we are all looking out our windows to see what story will be told.

We are not afraid, only afraid that no one will be watching.

In times such as these, there is only one thing I can do.

Today at twelve noon Beijing time

If anyone is looking out their window onto Chang'an Avenue

They will see a man

White shirt

(*He finishes buttoning his white shirt.*)

Black pants

(*He dusts off his black pants.*)

Two bags

(*He readies his two bags.*)

In front of a line of tanks rolling down the block. A man who has been standing still his whole life.

The party will say he was no one.

And they will be correct.

My whole life, I had been taught that it was not my moment.

But now I see:

It has always been my turn.

(*The sound of a fax transmission. A high-pitched keening overtakes the stage as the fax machine transmits.*)

(*At the same time, there's a sharp rattling at the door, pounding. The door is broken down.*)

(*But* **WEN CHANG** *doesn't move. He stands still.*)

(*And we realize.*)

(We know this image.)

(We've seen it before.)

(It's the iconic image of Tank Man:)

(A Chinese man standing in front of a row of tanks in Tiananmen Square.)

(It's **WEN CHANG.** *Or it's not.)*

(But the figure stands.)

(And stands.)

(And stands.)

(It's a screen.)

End of Play